COSTUME
IN PICTURES

'Ready for the Party' (1866) by James Hayllar

Phillis Cunnington

COSTUME

IN PICTURES

The Herbert Press

© Phillis Cunnington 1964
Revised edition © Phillis Cunnington 1981

Revised edition first published in Great Britain 1981
by The Herbert Press Limited, 65 Belsize Lane, London NW3 5AU

Designed by Pauline Harrison

Computer type-set by Page Bros (Norwich) Ltd

Printed in United States of America

ISBN cased 0 906969 05 0

Distributed in the United States of America by
Universe Books, 381 Park Avenue South
New York, N.Y. 10016

Library of Congress Catalog Card Number: 80-54880

US ISBN: 0-87663-358-0

Contents

'Dress is one of the various ingredients
that contribute to the art of pleasing, and therefore
an object of some attention.'

Lord Chesterfield's advice to his son, 1778

Introduction

This is a brief descriptive and pictorial survey of British and American costume. The book ranges from medieval days to the early 20th century, and the illustrations are reproductions of contemporary paintings, drawings, photographs, etc., gathered from a wide variety of sources.

In the art of costume the nature of the materials, their form and colour, combine to indicate, mostly by symbols, certain ideas: 'Costume is far more revealing than nudity', wrote C. W. Cunnington in *The Art of English Costume*. Primitive man discovered that a distinctive garb could denote a tribal chief or a witch doctor and distinguish one sex from the other, thus expressing the ideas of social rank, occupation and sex appeal. Hence clothing, because it expresses ideas, has become the art we call costume or dress.

A series of costumes illustrating the modes of past centuries reveals that rank has usually been expressed by garments entailing varying degrees of physical discomfort, and sex appeal can be fortified by maintaining a marked difference between the costumes of the sexes. In women's costume there has been a perpetual oscillation between concealment and exposure, and devices, no matter how uncomfortable, have been welcomed if it was thought that they might enhance sex appeal.

Although each person tries to impress something of his own personality on the costume he wears, it is, in fact, less expressive of the individual than of his group. It tells of a fashion, a taste shared by a large number of people for a short space of time. The conception of adaptability of costume to suit any particular function or the age of the wearer only strengthened during the 19th century.

Men's fashions seem more original, women's more imitative. Women have perpetually revived fashions of the past; men sometimes seem unwilling to change what they have.

Viewing the costumes of our ancestors, we cannot but notice their apparent indifference to aesthetics. Successive fashions thought beautiful by one generation were often scorned by the next. They seem strange to us, only because the ideas they expressed seem strange.

The Middle Ages

In the late Saxon period, costume still bore traces of the classical style of dress, which was—for both sexes—a loose covering concealing the shape of the body.

The man's wardrobe consisted of a tunic, knee or ankle length, with long sleeves. Over this was worn a super-tunic, the long style indicating persons of rank. A square mantle or cloak was the outer garment. The legs were clothed in braies or loose-fitting drawers, which by the 12th century were merely an undergarment like the shirt. Phrygian bonnets were worn, but it was the fashion to go bare-headed.

Men in short tunics, one embroidered, with side vents (11th century)

Women's costume was basically very similar, but always long to the ankles. It consisted of a sleeved tunic worn over the smock (chemise), a super-tunic often embroidered, a large square mantle and a long head-rail, draping the head and shoulders and concealing the hair.

The 11th-century tunic for men was slightly more close-fitting and always worn with a girdle, under the super-tunic. Hooded cloaks were introduced towards the close of the century, and shoes of leather were shaped to the foot, distinguishing right from left.

The female tunic, now called the kirtle or gown, was always worn with a girdle under the super-tunic, and the head-rail was known as the coverchief or kerchief. The cloak or mantle was similar to the male garment, but always long and without a hood.

Woman in embroidered super-tunic
over kirtle, mantle and head-rail
or coverchief (10th–11th century)

The 12th century introduced variations in men's tunics. The body was often close-fitting and the front of the skirt slit open up to the girdle. Headgear was more varied, including a hood, as a separate entity with a cape or 'gorget', a small round cap, a coif and hats of varying size.

After 1100 the women's dress for ladies of rank began to mould the figure, and both kirtle and super-tunic might have tight sleeves ending in long hanging cuffs—a feature of this century. The hair, hitherto concealed, might be worn in two long plaits sometimes encased in silk sheaths. Hooded cloaks were worn towards the end of the century.

Drawing of Young Offa (second from left) in a long cote
and typical 13th-century sleeves

A characteristic feature of the 13th century for both sexes was the cut of the sleeves, which were made in the 'Magyar' style, being very loose under the arm. The male tunic, now generally called the cote, might have a front vent to the skirt, and the super-tunic or surcote might be sleeveless. Variations of the surcote were: (*a*) the tabard, consisting of front and back panels joined under the arms at waist level; (*b*) the garde-corps or herigaut, a long voluminous hooded garment with long hanging sleeves which had an arm-hole slit above; and (*c*) the garnache, which was of the tabard style but had elbow length cape-like sleeves.

10

Women in super-tunics with pendant cuffs, and (right) hair in silk sheaths (1120–50)

The female kirtle was long and often trained. A new headgear, the barbette and fillet, was typical of the 13th century, and continued into the 14th. In consisted of a white linen band passing under the chin, attached to the hair on either side above the ears and worn with a stiffened circlet of linen. Under this circlet the hair might be enclosed in a fret or reticulated caul, resembling a hair net but often made of goldsmithry. 'A frett of goold sche hadde next hyre her.' (Chaucer: *Legend of Good Women, Prologue, c* 1385.)

Bridegroom in a herigaut, bride in fur-lined mantle with barbette and fillet headgear (13th century)

LEFT Nobleman in long tunic or cote, mantle, and gloves (13th century)

In the 14th century the man's tunic or cote was gradually replaced by the gipon (later to become the doublet). It was close-fitting with a loose knee-length skirt. The tight sleeves were buttoned to the elbow, to match the buttons down the front of the garment. The surcote was replaced by the cotehardie, which had elbow-length sleeves with pendant flaps. In the second half of the century these were extended into long narrow streamers called tippets. The girdle or belt was worn below the

13

Men in tunics, one putting on a cotehardie (1340)

waist. Dagging (scalloping) of garments was common among the upper classes. Outer garments were the garnache with cape-like sleeves and tongue-shaped lapels, and the houppelande (1380–1450), which from *c* 1450 was called the gown. The houppelande had a high upright collar and, fitting the shoulders, fell in tubular folds to the ground when worn ceremonially; otherwise the length varied. The sleeves were close, or funnel-shaped widening enormously at the wrist, or 'bag-pipe' falling in a great pouch from the cuffs closed at the wrist.

The leg hose, made of stretchable material cut on the cross ('byesse'), were often parti-coloured (until 1420), and boots and shoes were piked, having long points stuffed with tow from 1395 to about 1410. 'Their shoes and pattens are snouted and picked' (*Eulogium Historiarum*, written *c* 1420).

Men in coifs; third from left wears a garnache,
second from right wears a herigaut (1264–5)

15

18

Women also wore the cotehardie, over the kirtle. A new over-garment was the sideless surcote (1360–1500) developed from the sleeveless super-tunic. It had large side openings from shoulders to hips revealing the close-fitting kirtle and girdle beneath. The front portion, sometimes decorated, was called the placard. Mantles were ceremonial or worn for warmth and even sometimes fur-lined. The garde-corps was also worn by women for warmth.

Stockings reached above the knee and were gartered above or below: 'Here hosen weren of fine skarlet redde ful straite y-teyed', Chaucer says of the Wife of Bath.

Lady in long gown
and wearing a wimple
(14th century)

LEFT Henry V in
ceremonial houppelande
(c 1415)

New headgear was worn. The goffered veil (much later descriptively called the 'nebula head-dress') was made up of half circles of linen frilled along the straight edge to form an arch round the face. The wimple—a piece of linen or silk swathed round the front of the neck and chin, the ends being pinned to the hair above the ears and worn with veil or fillet—was introduced about 1150, and worn till the mid-14th century. Shaved front hair was a new mode from about 1370 to 1480, as also was eyebrow plucking and face painting.

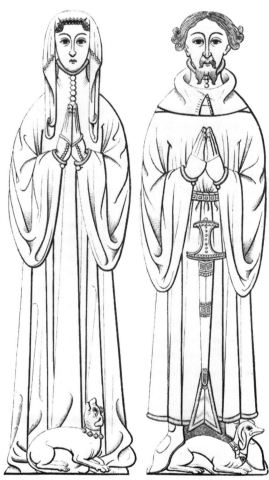

Long houppelandes with 'bag-pipe' sleeves (*c* 1400)

LEFT Bridegroom in low-belted houppelande,
bride in horned head-dress (*c* 1420)

21

One man in short jacket over doublet, the others in long gowns, wearing piked shoes (1470–80)

FAR RIGHT Short doublet, long hose with codpiece (1479–87)

In the 15th century the man's gipon, now called the doublet, was waisted and very short with close-fitting sleeves, and variously fastened down the front by buttons, lacing or, after about 1425, hooks and eyes. Eyelet holes in the doublet skirt were present for attaching the hose by means of strings known as 'points' which were passed through similar holes in the hose and then tied. This was known as 'trussing the points'.

The cotehardie, sometimes now called a jacket, was shortened, and the houppelande, long or short, was often trimmed with fur, usually belted at varying levels, made with a lower collar, and often with side vents in the skirt.

The hose in the form of long stockings was uncommon except for labourers. The long hose (from 1400 to 1515) were united at the top and continued up over the seat to form tights. A front flap at the fork

22

protruded as a small pouch known as the codpiece (*c* 1408–1575): 'A kodpese like a pokett' (*Townley Mysteries, c* 1460). Boots, shoes and pattens were worn, and by the end of the century began to be very square-toed.

Hats varied in shape, and the chaperon continued. The bowl-crop hair style was fashionable from 1410 to 1460, but subsequently a forehead fringe with hair to the nape of the neck or shoulders and a clean-shaven face became the mode.

After about 1450 the woman's kirtle was usually worn under the houppelande, which became her gown. From a rather high waist it fell in ample folds to the ground with a spreading train, the skirt sometimes measuring forty-five feet around the hem. The cotehardie, sideless surcote and ceremonial mantles were still worn.

24

Butterfly head-dress (1485)

Queen and one lady in sideless surcotes, the other three in gowns and heart-shaped head-dresses (1460–80)

25

Standing women in sideless surcotes, three seated figures in Turkey bonnets (*c* 1470–80)

A great variety of head-dresses were conspicuous during the second half of the 15th century. The so-called steeple head-dress was a French mode; in England a truncated cone was worn instead. The butterfly head-dress, *c* 1450–95, consisted of a wire frame supporting a gauze veil which spread out over the head like a pair of wings. It was fixed to a fez-shaped cap worn at the back of the head. V-shaped rolls rising above the forehead and curving each side over ornamental bosses called templers, were popular in the first half of the century, and were greatly heightened in the second half as horned head-dresses. 'Turkey bonnets'—any tall cylindrical brimless hats—were worn by both sexes and continued into the 16th century. Hair was entirely concealed except by a queen at her coronation, brides, children and sometimes unmarried girls.

The costume of the peasantry remained almost unchanged throughout the medieval period, consisting of shirts or tunics, breechclouts and/or hose. Women wore longer tunics and married women wore their hair covered with caps or veils. Materials were rough and simple, to suit the hard lives of the peasants.

The 16th century

Men, first half of the 16th century

Throughout the 16th century fashions of both sexes seem to emphasise social rank. A mass of new textiles and costly imports, their use restricted by sumptuary laws to the upper classes, combined to produce new standards of luxury. If size is a measure of importance, the male costume achieved this by means of padding known as bombast, and the female costume after 1545 by means of the hooped under-skirt known as the farthingale. In 1589 George Gascoigne wrote:

> Thy bodies bolstered out
> With bumbast and with bagges
> Thy roales, thy ruffs, thy cauls, thy coifes,
> Thy jerkins and thy jagges.

And in 1593 Nashe said that men 'shew the swelling of their mind in the swellings and plumping out of their apparel'. Decoration was extremely fashionable. A popular device was slashing—that is, the making of short or long slits (the latter called panes), through which decorative under-garments could be drawn out on view. Very short slashes were called pinking. Embroidery, especially in the form of black-work, that is embroidery in black silk, usually at the neck and wrist of shirts, was a feature from about 1530 for a hundred years.

During the first half of the century the man's main garment was his doublet, under which he might wear an under-doublet called a waistcoat, and over which he usually wore a jerkin or a gown. The doublet at first was low-necked, but after 1540 it had a standing collar. Above this appeared the shirt frill which later developed into the ruff. The doublet might be worn open at the neck to show the shirt, possibly embroidered with black-work which would be repeated on the shirt-sleeve frills at the wrist.

The jacket or jerkin worn over the doublet was sometimes paned or pinked and generally sleeveless or made with short shoulder sleeves or, from 1545, given wings—stiffened bands projecting over the shoulders like epaulettes. From 1540 the jerkin had a high-standing collar.

Male leg-wear comprised upper stocks, i.e. the breeches portion, now slightly ballooned and often paned, which continued down as nether stocks (the stocking portion), forming one garment. It was attached to

(left) Man in long gown, broad shoes (1507)

(right) Lady in gown and English hood, style of 1500

the doublet by ties, or 'points', as in the 15th century. If these gave way, 'Their points being broken, Down fell their hose' (Shakespeare: *I Henry IV*). Shoes, often slashed, had broad square toes until about 1540, after which they were rounded.

During the first half of the century small round caps called bonnets,

Buff jerkin, pinked, with stand collar and short sleeves (1550)

Henry VIII in long-skirted doublet, flat cap; Queen in gown and kirtle and English hood (*c* 1544)

RIGHT Prince Edward in doublet, over it a gown with hanging sleeves, and a flat cap (*c* 1545)

with close upturned brims, were usual. From the 1530s the most popular headgear was the flat cap 'couched fast to the pate, like an oyster' (A. Boorde). It had a flat crown, waisted on to a small flat brim, and was usually trimmed with one feather.

Paned sleeveless jerkin, small feather-trimmed bonnet (1547)

LEFT Doublet worn open to show black-work embroidery on shirt, with short gown (*c* 1548)

Women, first half of the 16th century

Women's costume in the 16th century was always listed as gown and kirtle. The kirtle, a front-fastening frock, was usually worn under the gown and over the smock. When worn alone it resembled a gown.

The gown was the more important article of dress. During the first half of the century it could be loose, but more commonly it fitted the figure, falling in ample folds to the ground and usually trained. The sleeves were close-fitting at the shoulder, widening greatly to the elbow. The kirtle sleeve appeared at the aperture or was a detachable sleeve closed at the wrist. Some gowns had short puffed shoulder sleeves, with or without sham hanging sleeves in the form of streamers. In some the sleeves were tight to the wrist with a puff at the shoulder or with wings.

Early form of English hood showing the hair (1501)

Many had skirts with a ∧-shaped opening in front showing a decorative panel, called the forepart, of the under-skirt or kirtle.

The low neck of the gown might be filled in by a partlet, which was usually decorative and had a collar edged with a frill that later developed into the ruff. 'A partlet of white satin garnished with gold...He cannot make a standing collar for a partlet without the measurement of her neck' (Henry VIII, Letters and Papers, 1533). Partlets and detachable sleeves often matched and made useful gifts.

Women's headwear was very distinctive. The coif, a simple linen cap tied under the chin, was worn indoors and often used as an undercap. The English hood, descriptively called the gable or pediment head-dress because of the pointed arch framing the face, fell in folds behind and

LEFT French hood with upper and nether billiments (*c* 1530)
RIGHT English hood, hair covered by striped 'rolls' (1520s)

had embroidered or jewelled lappets crossing the head and falling low on each side. After 1525 these lappets were often turned up and the curtain behind replaced by two broad, stiffened, hanging flaps. These, too, were sometimes turned up on to the crown. The hair previously seen under the arch was now concealed in silk sheaths, usually striped, rising to a point, and filling up the space under the arch of the head-dress.

The French hood (1520s–1590 and unfashionably to *c* 1630) was small and rounded, made on a stiff frame and worn far back on the head

Family group, *c* 1527:
the lady on extreme left
is wearing a lettice cap

exposing the hair. It was ornamented with two rows of jewels known as upper and nether billiments (billiments were also worn separately as head ornaments). A stiff ruched edging bordered the front of the hood, and the pendant tail behind was in one piece. When turned up, the pendant was worn flat on the head projecting over the forehead and was known as a bongrace (*c* 1530–1615). The bongrace was also a separate article pinned on, its purpose being to protect the face from the sun. The lettice cap, of fur resembling ermine, covered the ears with its side pieces and was worn over a coif.

37

Close-fitting gown, small ruff and French hood with bongrace (*c* 1550)

RIGHT Gown with double sleeves; English variation of French hood (*c* 1550)

Fur-faced ceremonial gown,
flat cap (1569)

RIGHT Pinked sleeveless jerkin
with high collar (1568)

Men, second half of the 16th century

In the second half of the century the male doublet was padded, 'bombasted' and stiffened with buckram. From *c* 1575–1600 the point in front at the waist was made to bulge forward with padding to form what was known as the peascod belly. Doublet skirts were short, often tabbed, and sleeves headed by wings were often detachable, the ties being hidden under these shoulder pieces.

The jerkin was generally sleeveless or merely winged. 'A common garment daylye used such as we call a jerkin or jackett without sleeves' (Thynne: *Animadversions,* 1599). Like the doublet it developed a high-stand collar.

The cloak for outdoor wear was very fashionable; the cassock, a loose short jacket, less so. A fur-trimmed gown was often ceremonial or worn by older men.

A doublet with peascod belly,
Venetians with stockings
gartered over them (1580–90)

LEFT Matching doublet with
peascod belly and Venetians,
and cartwheel ruff (1588)

41

42

Leg-wear varied. Trunk hose consisted of the upper portion, now distended with bombast, joined to the stocking portion, or with thigh-fitting extensions called canions over which separate stockings were pulled. Knee breeches were introduced in 1570 and, whether close fitting or baggy, were called Venetians.

Tall hat, embroidered ruff (1578)

LEFT Short cloak, doublet, trunk hose with canions, stockings pulled up over them. Mules on feet (1582)

Neck-wear comprised at first a turned-down collar called a falling band attached to the neck of the shirt, or with the frill surmounting the tall shirt collar. But by 1560 this frill had developed into a ruff which soon spread into a large separate article tied on by strings. The larger ruffs, e.g. the cart-wheel ruff (1580–1610), had to be supported on wire frames. All ruffs were stiffened with starch. Between 1580 and 1615 ruffs and falling bands might be worn together, the ruff surmounting the band (i.e. a turn-down collar).

Headgear was low and flat until about 1570, when the crown shot up into the shape known as the copotain or sugar-loaf hat, 'sometimes

43

Doublet with wings, trunk hose, ruff and falling band worn together (c 1595)

standying a quarter of a yarde above the crowne of their heads . . .as please the fantasies of their wavering mindes.' (P. Stubbes: *Anatomie of Abuses*, 1583).

Shoes had rounded toes and flat heels. Mules, called pantofles, were also worn. High riding boots with turn-over tops were now fashionable.

Women, second half of the 16th century

Women's dress in the second half of the century introduced the novelty of bodice and skirt as separate articles, the skirt alone now being styled the kirtle. The bodice was tight-fitting, with a short point at the waist. The neck was high or low; but if low, was usually filled in with a partlet and ruff. The sleeves became close-fitting, often with a puffing at the shoulders. Some had short shoulder sleeves with sham hanging sleeves and close-fitting sleeves of a different material from that at the wrist.

From 1580 the front of the bodice was open and filled in by a decorative stomacher. The sleeves expanded into a shape called trunk or cannon sleeves, generally having wings. The skirt was often open in front to expose an ornamental under-skirt or panel. The shape of the expanding kirtle depended on that of the hooped petticoat called the farthingale. The Spanish farthingale, from about 1545, was pyramidal or domed.

Close-bodied gown,
short oversleeves and sham
hanging sleeves (1562)

High-necked partlet,
gown edged with fur (*c* 1555)

45

Town and country folk (*c* 1570)

From 1560 it was replaced by the French farthingale, which was tub-shaped and under which was tied a padded bolster called a 'bum-roll'. In 1580 the wheel farthingale appeared, over which the skirt spread horizontally from the waist to fall vertically over the edge. In *c* 1590, to avoid the hard circular line thus produced at the circumference, the skirt was given a frilled border and became known as a frounced farthingale skirt.

For warmth or ceremony a gown was worn. It was loose or close-fitting, and sleeves, if present, were short and puffed. The principal

neck-wear was the ruff, which for women might be worn open in front. The fan-shaped ruff (1570–1625) was worn with a low neck by the unmarried, the ruff rising up from the sides and back of the decolletage to spread out fan-wise at the back of the head. At the wrists hand-ruffs or turned-back cuffs of lawn or lace were worn.

Headwear included hoods, hats and caps. The Marie Stuart hood was a small hood of lawn edged with lace, its front border dipping over the forehead. Hats and bonnets were worn for riding and the copotain was also worn by women. 'English burgher women usually wear high hats covered with velvet or silk.' (Platter: *Travels in England,* 1599). Indoor caps and jewelled cauls were worn, but it was quite correct for younger women, even out of doors, to go bareheaded.

Gown with partlet, wings to sleeves which match the forepart; billiment head ornament (1575–80)

Elizabeth I in frounced farthingale skirt, with cannon sleeves and hanging sleeves (1592)

Shoes were flat-heeled. Stockings were now being knitted.

The upper classes were clothed mainly in silks and velvet, leaving woollens for their inferiors. 'When your posterity shall see our pictures, they shall think wee were foolishly proud of apparel.' (Verstegan: *Antiquities concerning the English Nation*, 1605).

49

The 17th century

Male costume in the 17th century had four phases. Until the end of James I's reign it remained bulky in the Elizabethan tradition. Under Charles I a slimmer elegance was adopted and, although extreme Puritan and Cavalier dress had their different characteristics, 'The leaders and

their wives were as well dressed on the one side as on the other.'
(*Memoirs of the Life of Colonel Hutchinson*, by his Widow, Lucy).

The Restoration of Charles II (1660) introduced extravagant modes
from France, but some of these did not spread beyond the Court circle.
By 1680 experiments in better cut and fit were being attempted, made
possible by the wider use of woollen cloth by all classes.

LEFT Short-skirted doublet, compound ruff and bombasted breeches (*c* 1605–6)
CENTRE James I in Dutch breeches, copotain hat; Queen in wheel farthingale,
open ruff with neck frill (1605)
RIGHT Doublet with winged sleeves, short trunk hose joined to nether stocks;
shoe-roses (1616)

51

Men, first half of the 17th century

In the first half of the century the man's doublet, close-fitting with tight sleeves and wings, was short-skirted with square tabs. These tabs were lengthened after about 1610, dipping to a sharp point in front. The peascod belly ceased to be fashionable. After about 1630 the doublet became high-waisted and easy-fitting with deep skirts, and after 1640 it resembled a loose unwaisted jacket, the skirt represented by a series of shallow tabs or merely a tabbed border.

The jerkin, as a civilian garment, was discarded after 1630. Worn over the doublet it was sleeveless or made with wings, or with wings and hanging sleeves. The leather jerkin popular from 1620 to 1665 was made of ox hide, dressed with oil.

Short-skirted doublets, winged sleeves, full trunk hose (1617)

Leg-wear was extremely varied. Venetians continued rather unfashionably until 1620, as also did trunk hose which, however, were much longer, ending just above the knee with short canions completely covered by the hose. The codpiece was discarded. Trunk hose of the earlier style, without canions but joined to long stockings, were worn ceremonially to a later date. Dutch breeches, resembling shorts, were

52

Charles I in doublet and cloak-bag breeches trimmed with ribbon loops (1631)

Winged jerkin with sham hanging sleeves; cloak-bag breeches (1625)

A fop of 1645. Skimpy doublet, Dutch breeches trimmed with ribbon loops and aglets (ornamental metal tags). Coiffure with love locks, and face patches

RIGHT Sleeveless leather jerkin, falling ruff (*c* 1625)

fashionable up to about 1610; a wider style revived between 1640 and 1670. These were sometimes called slops if made very wide, a term applied also to baggy breeches. Cloak-bag breeches (1600s–1630s) were full, oval-shaped and gathered in above the knee, where they were often trimmed with decorative points or ribbon loops. Spanish hose (*c* 1630–45) were long-legged breeches narrowing towards the knee and ending below, where these, too, were usually trimmed with ribbon loops.

Cloaks for outdoor wear were fashionable until 1670. The gown was relegated to the learned professions, state officials and the elderly.

For neck-wear the standing ruff sewn to a tall neck band in several

Falling ruff and fashionable 'Roman T'
beard and moustache (1620–25)

Man in short, loose doublet, Spanish hose and sugar-loaf hat (1635–40)

goffered layers survived into the 1620s, but from 1615 to the 1640s the
falling ruff, generally compound, dropping downwards, was fashionable.
The band was the term for a collar. The falling band (1540s–1670s) was

a turn-down collar. During the 1630s it spread widely towards the shoulders. These collars were tied in front by band strings, as also were ruffs. The standing band (c 1605–1630) was a semi-circular collar, the curved portion standing up fan-wise behind the head, the straight edges meeting under the chin and there tied by band strings. This type was sometimes called a golilla.

Hats, worn indoors as well as out, were large and often feather-trimmed. Tall crowns predominated.

Man with French cloak;
woman in frounced farthingale gown,
long hanging sleeves, with Marie
Stuart head-dress (1613)

From 1600 shoes began to have raised heels and from c 1610 to 1680 very large rosettes called shoe-roses were a favourite form of trimming. Red heels were worn with full dress and for Court wear until the end of the 18th century.

Women, first half of the 17th century

Women continued to wear the farthingale until about 1625, though by 1615 it was often discarded. 'All the time I was at Court, I wore my green damask gown without a farthingale.' (Diary of Lady Anne Clifford, 1617).

The gown until about 1625 was low-necked and worn with a fan-shaped standing band or ruff open in front. A small neck frill of gauze

or lace inside the ruff was a 17th-century innovation, as also was the oval ruff from 1625 to 1650, which was never worn by men. This gown usually had hanging sleeves, from which the tight bodice sleeves emerged above the elbows.

Lady in gown with virago sleeves (1628)

LEFT Gown with jacket bodice and loose overgown; shoe-roses (1610–15)

From 1610 to 1615 a jacket bodice was worn, with the skirt falling in many folds to the feet. It was often worn with a loose overgown with hanging sleeves. The neck-wear was usually a golilla or a ruff.

Extreme décolletage exposing the breasts was a fashion for unmarried women between 1605 and 1650. 'Eye those rising mounts, your displayed breasts, with what shameless art they wooe the shamefast passenger.' (R. Braithwaite: *The English Gentleman and the English Gentlewoman*, 1641).

A new fashion after 1625 was a dress with a basqued jacket bodice and bulky sleeves, often paned and sometimes ballooned above and below the elbow, known as virago sleeves. With this style a favourite neck-wear was the whisk, a deep falling neckerchief generally trimmed

LEFT Lady in cassock, hood or
chaperone, and mask (1639)

Lady with a large neckerchief and muff,
wearing a mask (1640)

12

Country woman with apron
and closed oval ruff (1639–40)

with lace, 'called of most a gorget or falling whisk because it falleth
about the shoulders' (R. Holme: *Armourie*, 1688). The skirt was often
hitched up to show a decorative petticoat or under-skirt.

For outdoor wear, besides a cloak, a new garment called a cassock
was worn. This was a long loose overcoat with wide sleeves.

Muffs were carried by both sexes, and masks were often worn by
women to protect the face from the weather, especially when riding.
'She's mask'd and in her riding suit' (Lord Barry, Ram-Alley, 1611).

RIGHT Country woman wearing pattens (1640)

Lady with breasts exposed,
wearing a safeguard (1620–25)

Another riding accessory was the safeguard, which was a skirt or half skirt worn for warmth and to protect the dress from dirt when travelling. 'I bought a cloak and safeguard of cloth . . . to keep me warm on my journey.' (Diary of Lady Anne Clifford, 1616).

Hats were tall-crowned and large-brimmed. Small hoods called chaperones were also worn, but to go bareheaded out of doors was fashionable throughout the century. Patches were worn by women through the 17th and 18th centuries.

Charles II in petticoat breeches trimmed with 'fancies', stockings with deep flounces (cannons); Queen with trained over-skirt and virago sleeves (1662)

Men, second half of the 17th century

In the second half of the 17th century, after a short spell of extravagant modes brought over from France by Charles II, the male costume was simplified and it is customary to regard the modern style of man's dress as originating from the reign of Charles II, when the suit comprised coat, waistcoat (or vest) and breeches.

The doublet survived until about 1670. It was worn with petticoat breeches, introduced by Charles II but not popular with Englishmen. They were in the form of a divided skirt, each leg being so wide that Pepys wrote in 1661 of his friend who 'told of his mistake the other day, to put both his legs through one of his knees of his breeches and went so all day.' (April 6th). These breeches, also called Rhinegraves or pantaloons (1660s), were usually trimmed with masses of ribbon loops

LEFT Man in loose coat with short sleeves and shoulder knot; loose breeches gathered in at the knees (1670s)

RIGHT Fashionable youth wearing a cravat (1676)

called 'fancies', which often also bordered a wide form of shorts, discarded soon after the 1670s.

With the petticoat breeches and breeches unconfined at the knees were worn short stockings with deep flounces called cannons (not to be confused with canions).

After 1665 the jerkin and doublet began to be replaced by coat and waistcoat. These were cut on similar lines, being at first loose, unwaisted and hanging to the knees. The pockets were placed very low. The coat sleeves had turn-back cuffs and at first were often only elbow length, showing the elegant shirt sleeve. Gradually the sleeve was lengthened, and by 1690 the coat was made close-fitting and waisted with a flared skirt, the length being unaltered but pockets placed higher. The shoulder knot was a bunch of ribbons attached to the right shoulder as a form of decoration and was very popular from c 1660 to 1700.

Leg-wear now comprised breeches with fairly full 'bloomer' legs closed above or below the knee by strap and buckle. Sash garters below the knee were fashionable.

For outdoor wear, greatcoats and also a form of greatcoat called a Brandenburg (1674-c 1700) were the mode. This was long and loose and fastened with frogs and loops. Cloaks were worn for comfort, but were not fashionable.

After 1670 the falling band was replaced by the cravat, a neck-cloth of linen or muslin, the pendant ends usually trimmed with lace. Hats continued with wide brims, lower crowns, and in about 1690 the three-cornered or tricorne hat was introduced, to become the hall-mark of the 18th century. Hair was worn long, but after 1660 wigs began to replace the natural hair, and these were *de rigueur* at Court. After 1660 boots were less fashionable and chiefly worn on horseback.

Women, second half of the 17th century

In the second half of the 17th century women's gowns were long and tight-waisted, and if not closed at the neck the décolletage was low and circular. The skirt was usually trained and open in front, revealing a decorative under-skirt.

Gown with circular décolletage. Hair style typical of the period (1660–70)

Capes, tippets and scarves were worn out of doors, and large hats or small limp hoods were the head-wear. Indoors a fashionable innovation was the fontange (1690–1710), consisting of wired-up lace frills standing erect above the head and attached to a small close-fitting linen cap with two long lace streamers.

Shoes had high raised heels. Clogs were soles with straps for fastening over the shoes, and generally of a matching pattern. Pattens were worn by the less elegant and were 'a wooden shoe with an iron bottom' (*The Ladies Dictionary*, 1694).

Large hat worn over a coif, and
a neck whisk (1660–70)

Boy in flared waisted coat holding a tricorne hat; girl with sham hanging sleeves, wearing a fontange (1690)

The 18th century

Men, first half of the 18th century

During the first half of this century the components of a man's suit were often of the same material: cloth for day, and silk or satin, laced and embroidered, for evening or ceremonial wear. The collarless coat, close-fitting and waisted, had a flared skirt to the knees with back vent and two pleated side vents headed by 'hip buttons'. It was buttoned down the front to the hem until *c* 1735 or to the waist from 1720 on. Pocket flaps began to be scalloped from 1710. Vertical pockets were rare after 1720.

Low-necked coat, buttons to hem; roll-up stockings (1715)

RIGHT Flared coat buttoned to hem, with flapped pocket; full-bottomed wig (1710–20)

FAR RIGHT Flared coat, buttoned to waist, with scalloped pocket flaps (*c* 1725)

Coats with boot sleeves or boot cuffs (1730)

BELOW RIGHT Man in a campaign wig. Waistcoat worn open to show ruffles of shirt (1727)

FAR RIGHT Coat with slit cuffs, embroidered waistcoat, breeches buckled over the stockings (1735)

Sleeve cuffs varied and were usually large, closed or open behind, and sometimes falling away from the sleeve. The boot cuff typical of the 1730s was closed, elbow-length and so commodious that 'These boot-sleeves were certainly intended to be receivers of stolen goods.' (H. Fielding: *The Miser*, 1733). Some sleeves might be without cuffs, having a short side slit, buttoned.

The frock was an 'undress', i.e. informal, coat distinguished by its flat turn-down collar and no lapels. Borrowed from the artisan, it was worn from 1730 on, not only for comfort indoors but also for riding, sport and sometimes dancing.

The waistcoat or vest was cut like the coat but without pleated side vents. It was sleeved until the 1750s, and sometimes double-breasted, but often left open to display the frilled shirt front. The shirt ruffles (frills) at the wrist were always evident.

Knee breeches were universally worn throughout the century, buckled below the knee and either buttoned down the front without a fly until 1750, or from 1730 closed by front flaps called 'falls'. Long stockings

71

Man in banyan, night cap and
slippers (c 1740)

Low-necked coat and waistcoat
with slit cuffs (1739)

called roll-ups were worn, drawn up over the knee of the breeches, until mid-century, though breeches were being buckled over the the stockings by the 1730s.

For negligée the banyan or Indian night-gown resembling a loose knee-length coat, wrapping over in front, was very popular.

For neck-wear, the cravat continued into the 1740s. The Steinkirk from *c* 1692 to 1730 was merely the cravat twisted on itself and threaded through a button-hole of the coat. The stock from 1735 on was a high, stiff, made-up neckcloth of linen or cambric, buckled or tied behind. The solitaire (1730s–70s) was a black tie worn over the stock, variously arranged in front and usually worn with a bag wig.

The principal outdoor garment was the surtout, a greatcoat with a broad cape-like collar which, after 1730, was often called a 'wrap-rascal'. Cloaks were also worn. The roquelaure was a knee-length cloak with a single or double cape-collar.

Rider wearing a frock and top boots (*c* 1745)

Man in a frock, woman wearing a mob cap, child in a round-eared cap (1740–2)

Man wearing a Steinkirk cravat and
full-bottomed wig (*c* 1710)

Tennis player in short coat
and night cap (1705–20)

Shoes had square-blocked toes, high square heels and high tongues
till about 1740, when toes were rounded and heels and tongues made
lower. Buckles were small, increasing in size after the 1740s. Jack boots
with bucket tops or half jack boots, ending below the knee, were worn
on horseback only.

The three-cornered cocked hat, later descriptively called tricorne, was
worn throughout this period, but was frequently carried under the arm
owing to the universal wearing of wigs. The round hat was less common.
With a rigid brim it was worn by the learned professions; with a flopping

74

or 'slouched' brim, by youths. Night caps were worn over the shaved head for comfort, when the wig was discarded during the day and at night for warmth.

Wigs were worn by all classes, with or without a queue (the term used for the lock of hair hanging down behind), the size diminishing by the middle of the century. Dress wigs were always powdered white or grey. 'His wig had a pound of hair and two pounds of powder in it.' (Mrs Centlivre: *The Gamester*, 1705). The full-bottomed wig worn until *c* 1730, and subsequently only by the elderly, the learned professions and at Court, was a mass of curls framing the face and falling around the shoulders. It rose high above the forehead on each side of a centre parting, and was very costly. 'A full bottomed wigg £22' (*Book of Nicholas Carew*, 1705). The campaign or travelling wig, popular until *c* 1750, was similar but less cumbersome, having two short queues falling on each side in front and a corkscrew curl behind. The bob wig worn by all classes was always an undress wig. The long bob covered the neck, the short exposed it. From 1730 the toupee or foretop was introduced, whereby the front hair was brushed back into a roll above the forehead, eliminating the parting. It was plastered up with pomatum and the whole wig well powdered. 'Fear to put on this hat lest he should depress his foretop.' (S. Richardson: *Pamela*, 1740). The tie wig or pig-tail had a long queue interwoven with black ribbon. It was undress but smart. The bag wig, or merely 'bag', worn throughout the 18th century, was a dress or full dress wig. The queue was concealed in a square black silk bag with a stiff black bow at the nape of the neck.

Swords were carried by gentlemen, but from 1730 these were being replaced by long malacca canes.

Among the working classes and for sport, coats and waistcoats tended to be short and sleeves were without cuffs (see tennis player, opposite).

Women, first half of the 18th century

Throughout the 18th century a woman's dress usually comprised a gown and petticoat. The gown consisted of bodice and skirt in one, the skirt being open in front to reveal the petticoat, which was an essential part of the dress and not an under-garment. For convenience this style is called an open robe. The term petticoat was often confusingly shortened to 'coat', and petticoat or coat indicated a woman's skirt and not necessarily the under-garment. The term 'skirt' in the 18th century was almost wholly confined to the skirt of a man's coat. Some gowns were

75

Lady in open robe over oblong hoop, wearing a round-eared cap and holding a bergère hat (1743–5)

LEFT Lady in open robe with stomacher and robings, quilted petticoat, wearing a pinner (1741)

closed robes not requiring the petticoat. Another style was a separate bodice and skirt, the bodice or jacket falling outside the skirt or petticoat. Gown bodices varied in detail only, until the last quarter of the 18th century. Until then low necks and short sleeves were universal. The hang of the skirt depended on the underwear. A bustle was worn until about 1710 and again from 1775 to the 1790s, when it became very small.

The hoop or hoop-petticoat, *c* 1710–80 and for Court wear until 1820,

was variously distended with cane, wire or whalebone. The shape also varied. The bell hoop, worn throughout the hoop period, was dome-shaped; the fan hoop, 1740s and 1750s, was pyramidal; the oblong hoop, very wide from side to side, was fashionable from the 1740s to 1760s.

The bodice of the open robe was itself often open and filled in by a decorative panel called a stomacher, the join being covered by bands of flat ruchings called robings. Sleeves were elbow length, with turned up cuffs till *c* 1750, or ruffles from 1740.

Lady in wrapping gown (1740)

LEFT Lady in sack-back gown, treble sleeve flounces and bergère hat (1750)

The skirt was trained until 1710, when trains went out of fashion until 1760, except for mantuas and Court wear. The mantua was a loose gown with unboned bodice and, like the night-gown which was an open robe with covered neck, was worn on all occasions.

Of closed robes, later known as round gowns, the two main styles were: (1) the wrapping gown of *c* 1708–50, which had a wrapover front, and a low neck filled in by a lace surround called a tucker and a 'modesty piece' crossing the bosom; (2) the sack, originating from France, which was popular in England from 1720 to 1780 but after *c* 1750 became an open robe. The essential feature of the latter was the sack-back, miscalled the 'Watteau Pleat': two box pleats, single, double or treble, stitched

down from the back of the neck to the shoulders and thence left loose to merge with the fullness of the skirt. The fall of the skirt depended on the style of hoop in fashion.

The third style of dress, comprising separate bodice and skirt, had three main types of bodice: the jacket (French, *casaquin*), figure-fitting with short basques; the petenlair (1740s to 1770s), a loose thigh-length jacket with a sack-back; and the riding habit, which had a jacket resembling a man's and was worn with a waistcoat and petticoat (i.e. skirt).

Of neck-wear, besides the tucker and modesty piece, a fuller covering was the handkerchief or neckerchief. (In the 18th century the word 'handkerchief' for women meant neck-wear unless pocket-handkerchief was specifically stated.) This was a square of silk, gauze, muslin or linen, folded diagonally and swathed round the neck to a V in front. The cravat and Steinkirk were worn by women on horseback and were often brightly coloured. 'To a green Steinkirk £1. 1. 6' (Mist's *Weekly Journal*, 1708). Elegant aprons without bibs were worn as decorative additions to women's dress.

Outdoor garments were all in the nature of cloaks, the only covering possible with the fashions of this period. There were variations with different names. The mantle was a long tent-like garment always worn with a hood. The mantlet, coming into fashion in the 1730s, was a deep shoulder cape. The scarf was a deep wrap like a cape, with long ends falling in front. The manteel was a small edition of the scarf, and the fur tippet or palatine was similar but made of fur, usually with a matching muff.

Women's heads in the 18th century were normally covered, indoors as well as out. A 'head' was the general term for a head-dress worn indoors. 'Lost; a Head with very fine looped lace' (*Protestant Mercury*, 1700). The fontange from 1690 survived till about 1710. The pinner, *c* 1700–40, was a circular linen cap edged with a frill and worn flat on the head (as well as the name for the bib of an apron). Two long streamers called lappets were optional.

The round-eared cap, *c* 1730–60s, was coif-shaped, curving round the face to the ears and edged with a frill. The mob cap, never 'dress' wear, was worn throughout the century. 'The ladies were all in mobs . . . undrest' (J. Swift: *Journal to Stella*, 1710). Usually of cambric or muslin,

Lady wearing a petenlair (*c* 1745)

it had a high puffed-up caul and frilled border. Until 1750 it was bonnet-shaped with side lappets loose or tied under the chin and called kissing strings or bridles. Plain mobs were worn in bed and called night caps. The pompon, 1740s–60s, was a head ornament of ribbon, lace, feathers or tinsel, worn instead of, or with, a cap.

Indoor day caps were frequently worn out of doors, alone or under other headgear. Out of doors, hoods, short or long and variously named, were worn throughout this period, as also were rather low-crowned hats with narrow or wide flopping brims. The bergère or shepherdess hat of

LEFT Lady in riding habit wearing a Steinkirk cravat and carrying a tricorne (1720)

RIGHT Ladies wearing mobs, one with kissing strings (1733)

BELOW Lady in closed robe over bell hoop, wearing a pompon (1745–50)

straw with a wide brim was popular in the 1730s, when rusticity was the fashion, and was worn off and on to the end of the century. The tricorne hat was worn by women only on horseback, and usually over a wig. Hair ceased to be raised above the forehead after 1710, when hair styles became very plain and fairly smooth, except for the *tête de mouton* (1730s–1750) which consisted of short curls, real and false, behind and one on each side. Rouge, powder, eyebrow-plucking and patches were all fashionable accessories of the toilet.

Shoes had massive high heels and pointed toes, and the tongues were high and square until *c* 1750. Elegant over-shoes called clogs were often made to match the shoes. Pattens with wooden soles raised on iron rings, as in the second half of the 17th century, continued to be worn in wet weather, mostly by social inferiors.

> The milk-maid safe through driving rains and snows
> Wrapp'd in her cloke and propp'd on pattens goes.
> (Soame Jenyns: *The Art of Dancing*, 1730)

Men, second half of the 18th century

The side seams of the coat were increasingly curved back, bringing the hip buttons closer together and narrowing the back. At the same time the front skirts were cut back, eliminating, in the 1760s, the flared skirts, which, by the 1790s, were reduced to squared coat-tails. This coat, with modifications, has survived for men's evening dress to this day. A narrow stand collar was added from 1769, which increased in height in the 1780s and 1790s. Sleeves were close-fitting with rather smaller round cuffs or made with a short buttoned vent. A new cuff from *c* 1740 was the mariner's cuff, which was crossed in front by a vertical flap with three or four buttons matching those on the coat.

The frock with its turn-down collar followed the cut of the coat but, being looser and more comfortable, gained favour and from the 1770s could be worn on all occasions except at Court, where, after 1785, a French frock with a high stand-fall collar was admitted. 'Egad . . . the stiffness of my cape [the 18th-century term for a turn-down collar] gave me a sense of the pillory.' (General Burgoyne: *The Hermit*, 1786). When the frock replaced the coat it was sometimes called a frock-coat.

A gentleman writing from Paris in 1752 said, 'I was so damned uneasy in a full-dressed coat with hellish long skirts . . . I frequently sighed for my little loose frock which I look upon as an emblem of our happy

Gentleman in coat with low stand collar. Raised and forked toupee to wig (1762)

constitution; for it lays a man under no uneasy restaint but leaves it in his power to do as he pleases.' (Arthur Murphy's *Gray's Inn Journal*, 1752). The frock was single-breasted until 1780, subsequently usually double-breasted with lapels. Inside pockets in the lining, replacing the outside flapped pockets, were introduced in 1777 by the ultra-fashionable young men known as Macaronis, 'travelled young men' back from Italy.

The waistcoat, now sleeveless, became increasingly short, and by the 1780s was usually square cut without a slope away from the last button. A small stand collar was added in the 1760s, which was heightened in the 1780s to correspond with the coat. Double-breasted waistcoats were not popular until the 1780s, after which they were usual.

Breeches continued to be made on the same lines, though in the 1750s it was fashionable to have them buckled above the knees. Otherwise they were buckled below the knee or sometimes, in the 1780s, fastened with ribbon ties. Braces, called gallowses, were used from 1787. Pantaloons or close-fitting tights were introduced in the 1790s.

Coats were now increasingly made of cloth, breeches of buckskin and pantaloons of stockinette.

The negligée, night-gown or morning gown and banyan, continued
unchanged to the end of the century.

For neck-wear the cravat was going out of fashion, though revived
by the Macaronis in the 1770s. The stock was now the vogue and, like
the coat collar, increased in height and was sometimes stiffened with
pasteboard. 'My neck is stretched out in such a manner that I am
apprehensive of having my throat cut with the pasteboard.' (*Gentleman's
Magazine*, 1761). From *c* 1785 a stock formed of muslin, wound several
times round the neck and knotted in front, was again called a cravat.

For outdoor wear the surtout or greatcoat, large and loose and often
with several broad falling collars called capes, continued in use. Cloaks
were now reserved for the army, the learned professions and funerals.
The spencer, for men, appeared in 1790. It was a short-waisted jacket
with a stand-fall collar and cuffed sleeves. It was worn out of doors over
the coat or frock.

Shoes continued on the same lines, but heels were lowered in the
1760s, becoming very flat in the 1790s. Red heels were worn by beaux
until 1750, after which they were dress or Court wear until *c* 1760; then

they went out of fashion till 1770, when revived by Charles James Fox. Low shoes and mules were called slippers and were often of brightly coloured Morocco leather. Light jackboots were worn on horseback. Hessians appeared in 1795; these were short riding boots reaching to below the knee and rising slightly in front to be decorated with a tassel. Highlows, from 1785 on, were calf-length boots, laced in front and worn chiefly by labourers and country folk.

For head-wear the three-cornered hat with some variations in the cock remained the favourite, though from the 1770s on the round hat was slowly replacing it, especially for riding. It had a round brim and round flat crown which, from the 1780s, grew taller as the brim shrank. 'The hatter has of late years perpetually diminished the little brim he allows us' (*The Times*, 1799).

Wigs continued to be worn to the end of the century, but declined in fashion in the 1790s. The physical wig, from the 1750s, was a bushy long bob mostly worn by the learned professions, while the club or catogan, from the 1760s, had a club-shaped queue and was much favoured by the Macaronis in the 1770s.

Of accessories: gloves, muffs and walking sticks were carried by men and, in 1756, umbrellas for men were introduced by Jonas Hanway. These were, however, considered effeminate. Watches, too, were fashionable. 'All the very fine men wear two watches' (Diary of Mrs Philip Lybbe Powys, 1777).

Women, second half of the 18th century

Women's dresses fell into the same groupings as in the first half of the century until *c* 1794, when classical styles were introduced.

The sack was short in the 1750s.

> She wore her gear so short, so low her stays
> Fine folk shew all for nothing nowadays.
>
> (D. Garrick: Prologue to *Barbarossa*, 1755)

Trains came back for about a decade in the 1760s. The hang of the skirt again depended on the hoop, which, however, went out of fashion after 1780 except for Court wear. The Brunswick or German gown, 1760–1780, was a sack with long tight sleeves. The trollopee or slammerkin, *c* 1750–1770, was a loose unboned sack with a train and always an 'undress' worn for comfort. The confusing term 'night-gown' gradually

Gown with embroidered robings; round-eared cap (*c* 1750)

lost its negligée significance and might be worn in public. At a wedding breakfast it was stated that 'Soon after 11 o'clock Lady Mary's apparel was a nightgown of silver muslin with silver blond hat and cap' (Houblon family: Diary of Rev. S. Abdy, 1770).

From *c* 1770–85 the polonaise, an open robe in which the over-skirt was bunched up into about three puffs behind, was the height of fashion. This and the petticoat were short; but in the long polonaise, the over-skirt was trained and the sleeves usually long.

From 1784 to 1794 bodices of open robes were generally puffed out over the bosom with a buffon, a large diaphanous neckerchief, and the skirt, supported over a bustle, was trained. The separate bodice and skirt style was never dress wear, and the bodice was always in the form of a jacket. For riding, a waistcoat might be added.

LEFT Lady in short polonaise with parasol (1779)

RIGHT Lady in walking dress (1786)

92

From 1794 round gowns (meaning bodice and skirt in one) of the classical style became the mode. Often made of white materials, they were high-waisted, with long or short sleeves, and were worn with the minimum of underclothing. Aprons as dress accessories were discarded in the 1790s, when they were worn only for domestic use.

Open robe (left) with buffon neck fill-in (1784)

For outdoor wear cloaks in various forms continued to the end of the century. From 1750 to 1800 the pelisse was a capacious, cloak-like coat, with a hood or cape collar and vertical slits for the arms. Overcoats began to be worn in the 1780s when this was made possible by the absence of hoops.

Short-waisted, trained gown with long tight sleeves and buffon (1795–1800)

Lady (right) in a gown with long over-skirt, wearing a mob cap (c 1790)

Indoor caps were never discarded, though an attempt was made to dispense with them in the 1750s. Instead they shrank to a small size, and were usually worn under the outdoor hat.

Let the cap be mighty small
Bigger just than none at all.

(Francis Fawkes: His Mistress's Picture, 1755)

The mob cap varied in size, but was large in the 1780s, and from 1750
was without kissing strings. The dormeuse was a day cap despite its
name, with a puffed-up caul and deep side flaps called wings, popularly

Lady in wig of the period and wearing a buffon (*c* 1785)

RIGHT Large mob cap, plain neckerchief
and long tight sleeves (*c* 1792)

known as 'cheek wrappers'. It was sometimes tied under the chin.

Hats were fairly simple until the 1770s, when they became very large with a great variety of shapes. The hat immortalized by Gainsborough is one example; another is the lunardi or balloon hat (1783), which had a ballooned crown and a wide brim. The calash, from *c* 1770 to 1790, was a very large hooped folding hood, being built up on arches of whalebone or cane covered with silk. It was worn out of doors to protect the fashionable high coiffures from the weather.

These high coiffures of the 1770s and 1780s made large hats a necessity: the hair was piled up over cushions and rolls and sometimes wire supports, to a great height, which was increased by false hair and false

96

curls, the back hair hanging down in a flat loop or chignon or in longer curls. Adornments of flowers, vegetables and feathers might be added with plenty of scent and white or yellow powder:

> While the black ewes who own'd the hair
> Feed harmless on in pastures fair,
> Unconscious that their tails perfume,
> In scented curls, the drawing room.
>
> (William Whitehead, 1776)

In the 1790s hats and hair styles shrank. Ringlets, cropped hair or the Grecian style were the main types, with variations.

Shoes with high Louis heels, pointed toes and buckles disappeared in the 1790s, when ribbon rosettes replaced buckles and heels became quite flat. Short boots were worn out of doors.

Short polonaise, calash and pattens (1770s)

The 19th century

Men, first half of the 19th century

The collarless coat of the 18th century never returned to fashion, but the 18th-century frock, i.e. the tail-coat with stand-fall collar variously modified, continued throughout the 19th century. During the first half of this century the three components of a man's suit were generally of different materials and colours, the waistcoat usually being a striking feature. The 'suit of dittos', where all three were of the same material, was rare except in the country.

The tail-coat, which at first was day as well as evening wear, was a square cut-back with two coat-tails headed by hip buttons. The collar was a stand-fall with or without lapels. When these were present, the notch between lapel and collar was either an open V or an M cut. This M cut appeared in 1803 and was used until *c* 1855 for all coats and for evening dress into the 1870s. It is a good dating point for 19th-century coats; so is a seam at the waist which appeared first in 1823. The tail-coat might be double- or single-breasted and was worn on all occasions until the 1840s, when it was always a 'dress' coat. The coat collar varied in shape, and in the 1820s 'The collar ascends very high on the neck and the crease rolls over something like a horse-collar.' (Hearn: *Cyclopaedia of British Costume*, 1825).

Sleeves were long, ending at the wrist with a short buttoned vent or small cuff. Day coats varied in colour; the evening dress coat was usually dark blue with a velvet collar, though other dark colours were permissible, but the full dress was always black or blue.

The frock-coat, the hall mark of the 19th century, appeared about 1816, and differed completely from the 18th-century frock. It was a waisted close-fitting coat, at first single-breasted with a roll or small stand-fall collar and buttoned down to waist level. It had a full skirt hanging vertically in front, with a back vent, side pleats and hip buttons. In the 1820s lapels were added. The jacket came into fashion towards the end of the 1840s, but short sporting coats were worn much earlier (see page 105).

The waistcoat, single-breasted or double-breasted, was at first short, square cut with a stand collar. In the 1820s a roll collar was an alternative fashion, and by the 1840s waistcoats had flat lapels. The square-cut front gradually dipped to a slight point.

Leg-wear was now of three kinds: breeches, pantaloons and trousers. There were a number of euphemisms for men's trousers in the 19th century, ranging from 'inexpressibles', c 1800, and later 'unwhisperables', to 'nether integuments', 'don't mentions', 'unmentionables', 'bags' and 'kicksies'.

Breeches were full evening dress wear until the 1840s. But for riding and sport breeches were worn to the end of the century. The front closure was, as in the 18th century, a flap called a 'fall'. The fly front began to be used with ceremonial breeches soon after 1840.

LEFT Tail-coat with
M collar, pantaloons
and Hessians, and
a 'starcher' (1802)

Gentleman in early
form of frock-coat
(1818)

101

Man in morning suit with breeches (1800)

Pantaloons, inherited from the late 18th century, lasted until *c* 1850. Strapped pantaloons, having a strap under the instep to keep them in place, were worn from 1819 to the 1840s. Pantaloons for evening wear were short enough to show the stockings and were not strapped.

Trousers, though worn unfashionably from 1800, became fashionable from 1807, and black trousers could be worn with evening dress in the 1830s. They were close-fitting but did not outline the shape of the leg and, from the 1820s to 1850, and unfashionably later, they were usually strapped under the instep. Closure by front falls was the mode until *c* 1823, when the fly front fastening was introduced, gradually displacing the earlier method. Braces were used for breeches, pantaloons and trousers. The term gallowses survived among country folk to the mid-19th century, while the American term was 'suspenders'.

There were two main types of neckwear during the first half of the century, both generally termed a neckcloth. The cravat was now a large square neckerchief folded into a thick band and wrapped round the neck over the shirt collar with the ends tied in front. In the early years the shirt collar rose up above the cravat, with two points projecting on to the cheeks. 'Pray is it the fashion for the shirt collar to stand as high as the corners of the eyes?' (Lady Stanley: *The Early Married Life of Maria*

LEFT Evening dress, 1807; the gentleman holds a 'chapeau bras'

RIGHT 'Half full dress', 1808, the gentleman wearing trousers

103

M cut to collar; tight pantaloons with ankle slits (1804)

Josepha, 1800). Gradually the cravat, as it increased in height, was starched and arranged in many different ways and given as many names, a popular name being a 'starcher'. At Bath

> Each lordly man his taper waist displays,
> Combs his sweet locks and laces up his stays,
> Ties on his starched cravat with nicest care
> And then steps forth to petrify the fair.
>
> (*The English Spy*, 1825)

In the 1840s the cravat was scarf-like and tied or swathed over the shirt front. In contrast a very small cravat appeared, '. . . a bit of broad shoe-string to which the recherché name of "Byron tie" has been given' (*Punch*, 1843). The stock was a made-up stiffened neckband tied or buckled behind. It was far less popular than the cravat and was gradually relegated to sporting costume.

105

A greatcoat, top hat and
tight trousers (1818)

Morning suits, tail-coats,
strapped trousers (1843)

For negligée, dressing gowns were worn at breakfast, and the banyan, lasting to about 1850, was now essentially an indoor garment worn for comfort. 'I flew to my own bedroom where having discarded all my clothes but my shirt and my banyan, my Lord came and made me a visit in his banyan and slippers.' (Creevey: *Life and Times*, 1827).

Out of doors the greatcoat, single or double-breasted, was fashionable throughout. It was voluminous and long, and the style known as the box coat, with a number of capes and originally worn on the box of a coach, was also worn for walking. Cloaks were unfashionable except for evening dress and then often caped. The spencer survived with the elderly till about 1850. In the 1830s a very short greatcoat, without a seam at the waist, was called a paletot. Many other names and variations occurred at this time. The mackintosh appeared in 1836, being a short loose overcoat of Mackintosh's patent India-rubber cloth, for wearing in wet weather. But at first it met with much opposition owing to 'the offensive stench which they emit' (*Gentleman's Magazine of Fashion*, 1839).

Men's footwear indoors consisted of low-heeled slippers with short toe caps. Pumps with short quarters and low sides were worn with full dress. Outdoors a variety of boots was worn, including Hessians until 1850. The Wellington boot, which appeared in 1819, was a top boot without a turn-over top. Elastic-sided boots and button boots came into fashion in 1837. Shoes were tied by lachets over a central tongue. Gaiters were also worn.

On the head, the top hat was worn throughout the 19th century. The tall crown varied in height and slightly in shape, as did the shallow brim. Top hats were usually made of black silk, though in the early years beaver was used. Round hats with low crowns and wide brims were far less common; but in the 1830s this shape was adapted to be used as an opera hat, and known as the 'Circumfolding Dress Hat': 'the crowns are made to fold in the middle so as to be carried under the arm' (*Gentleman's Magazine of Fashion*, 1830).

The general wearing of wigs ended with the 18th century, though wigs with short queues were still occasionally worn.

Women, first half of the 19th century

The classical style of dress continued from the 18th century during the first decade of the 19th. The waist was high and the skirt, whether for day or evening, might be trained and was often of semi-transparent

Two evening dresses, one with feathered head-dress, and a day dress (1808)

material exposing the shape of the body or revealing the underclothes such as 'drawers of light pink now the "ton" among our dashing belles' (*The Chester Chronicle*, 1804). The term round gown now began to mean an untrained gown, while the frock was a dress with bodice and skirt joined. In 1815 gores were introduced so that the skirt was able to expand from a very short waist to a broadening base often only ankle length. The neckline was high or low and sleeves were long or short, except for evening dress when décolletage and short sleeves were the rule.

Bustles in the shape of large rolls tied under the back of the skirt as high as possible, from 1815 to 1819, gave rise to the fashionable 'Grecian bend'.

By 1824 the waist had descended to the normal level and tight lacing prevailed. Shoulders were widened by various types of sleeve and skirts

Lady in pelisse and cap, gentleman in greatcoat, top hat and Hessian boots; (right) lady in opera dress (1809)

expanded to a broader base. Sleeves had many names, the best known being the gigot or leg-of-mutton, from *c* 1825. It was very full above, gradually decreasing to the elbow and tight at the wrist. All the full sleeves were kept distended by pads, stiff linings or sometimes by whalebone hoops. Evening dresses had puffed shoulder sleeves and were always décolleté.

All through the 1830s the skirt continued to expand and the bustle in the form of a crescent-shaped cushion or a tier of stiff frills was worn. 'A waist like a wasp, a magnificent bustle' (Miss Mitford: *Our Village*, 1830). After 1836 the sleeve collapsed, especially at the shoulders, where the sleeve insertion was often lowered.

In the 1840s the bodice was very tight-fitting, often descending to a point in front, and the voluminous skirt was expanded over a larger bustle with multiple petticoats helping to give a dome-shaped appear-

109

Pelisse, worn with
straw bonnet (1825)

ance. This expansion was also helped by petticoats stiffened with crinoline, a material made of horsehair and wool. (The so-called crinoline or hooped petticoat did not appear until 1856). Sleeves were close-fitting, but a short bell-shaped expansion began to appear in 1843 which was the usual mode after 1848. These sleeves were finished by white detachable undersleeves to the wrist, usually trimmed with lace or embroidery and called engageantes.

Blue satin evening dress
and violet fur-lined
cloak (1824)

In the 1840s a jacket bodice with separate skirt, though worn previously, now became popular. Some were worn open with waistcoat fronts imitating a man's waistcoat.

Trimming with flounces, tucks and lace in various ways was used from 1800, but was very much the mode in the 1840s.

111

Neck-wear was very varied. A small ruff of lace was worn with both evening and day dresses into the 1830s. The habit-shirt, or chemisette, was a white muslin or cambric 'fill-in' to the bodice of a day gown cut low. The tucker was a strip of lace diminishing the décolletage and corresponding with the modesty piece of the 18th century. The half handkerchief was knotted loosely round the neck, and the tippet, of lace or lawn or sometimes swansdown, with long ends hanging in front, was worn with day or evening dress. The pelerine was a cape-like collar having pendant ends after 1825 and then often called a fichu pelerine. The bertha from the 1840s was a deep fall of lace or silk encircling the neck and shoulders, or merely the shoulders, worn with a low-necked evening gown.

Among outdoor garments was the pelisse, a form of overcoat occasionally called a greatcoat. It followed the cut of the dress of the period, and at first was short-waisted and long. In the 1820s the multiple cape was common. From c 1817 to 1850 it was often worn alone and then called a pelisse-robe or, after 1840, a redingote. The spencer was a short-waisted jacket which was very popular until the 1820s, when waists came down. A variety of cloaks, mantles and shawls were worn throughout this period.

Day and evening caps were still worn indoors, tending to be fairly small. These included mob caps, but the term was seldom used after 1830. Any indoor cap tied under the chin was known as a cornette. In the 1820s the size of all caps increased and shapes were very varied. The large evening beret was very popular in the 1820s, and towards the end of this period J. W. Croker, at a dinner party, seated between two of them wrote: 'Caught an occasional glimpse of my plate.' (*The Croker Papers*). But from the 1830s young women preferred hair decoration for evening wear.

Out of doors, hats and bonnets of varying shapes were worn, and these, too, grew larger with the expanding dress styles. The enormous hats and bonnets with high crowns and large brims of the late 1820s and 1830s were constant targets for ridicule. From 1830 bonnets had 'bavolets', i.e. short curtains shading the back of the neck. During the 1830s quillings of tulle or lace were sewn to the bonnet-strings so that, when tied, they formed a white frill round the chin; they were very popular and known as mentonnières or chin-stays. A small calash or caleche

Carriage dress, dinner dress and promenade dress (1830)

LEFT Evening
dress with 'Apollo knot'
hairstyle (1833)

Tight, pointed bodice and
dome-shaped skirt, with typical
1840s hairstyle (1843)

was revived in 1834 (see page 98). By the 1840s the bonnets were demure, surrounding the face; hats, except for riding, were rare.

Hair style during the classical period was worn short or with ringlets, often purposely dishevelled. Ringlets increasing in length and variously arranged continued to be fashionable, and in the 1840s they fell from a centre parting to the neck or bosom on each side of the face. These ringlets were frequently bought ready-made: 'long full ringlets—false of course—streamed down her fat red cheeks and rested on her shoulders' (R. S. Surtees: *Hillingdon Hall*, 1844). The Apollo knot, *c* 1824–33, was an extremely popular loop of false hair wired up to stand erect above the head with the evening and sometimes the day coiffure.

Rouge was used throughout this period.

On the feet, shoes in the form of slippers were worn indoors and out.

Short laced boots and elastic-sided boots were also worn, and rubber galoshes were used in muddy weather. In 1847 coloured silk boots or white ones with black toe caps became the fashion for evening dress.

Men, second half of the 19th century

'There are four kinds of coat which a well-dressed man must have; a morning coat, a frock coat, a dress coat and an over coat.' (*The Habits of Good Society*, 1855).

The frock-coat, 'so peculiar is the garment to England' (*The Gentleman's Herald of Fashion*, 1858), was by now the usual day coat for gentlemen, and in the 1870s a dress frock-coat appeared for formal occasions. Its rival was the morning coat, which sloped away from the front to broad tails behind, 'a half cut away, half frock' (*Twelve Inside and One Out*, 1855). It was sometimes called a riding or shooting coat.

The dress lounge, called a dinner jacket in 1896 or a tuxedo in America, was a welcome innovation in 1888 and could be worn for informal evening parties and dinners.

Frock-coat of the 1860s and morning coat of the 1870s

Double-breasted waistcoat with wide lapels (1860)

Mr Dickens in a short frock-coat, Mr Disraeli in a suit of dittos (i.e. all of one material) with lounge jacket (1870)

During this period comfort and flexibility were increasingly sought after and the jacket, generally termed the lounging or lounge jacket, steadily gained favour. There were a great many variations in named styles, the Norfolk jacket of the 1880s, called a Norfolk shirt in the 1870s, being the most striking and popular for all outdoor exercise. It was made with a box pleat down each side in front and a central box pleat behind, and from 1894 a yoke was often added. Pockets were large. It was commonly made of Harris tweed with a belt of the same material, and always worn with knickerbockers to match (see page 120).

Waistcoats throughout this period were short, double- or single-breasted and with or without lapels.

For leg-wear trousers were now the rule and instep straps were going out. American trousers 'gathered into a narrow waist band with pockets

Earliest form of dinner or dress jacket, or tuxedo in the USA (1889–90)

A caped Inverness (left) and a double-breasted Chesterfield (right) (1889)

in the side seams . . . worn without braces as the waist band may be fastened behind by buckle and strap' (Minister's *Gazette of Fashion*, 1857) came into fashion for day wear at the same time as the peg-top trousers. These were wide above, sloping down to a close fit at the ankles, and generally made with stripes or checks. 'Those stupid stripes down your trousers, what do you mean? Must you be marked all over like a giraffe?' (*Punch,* 1854). They were not very popular and went out of fashion about 1865. Evening-dress trousers were always narrower, and from the 1870s on were often made with braided side seams.

118

Gentleman's country costume, 1899: single-breasted lounge jacket, matching knickerbockers with box bottoms, ribbed stockings and short laced boots

Breeches were confined to sport and riding, but in the 1860s a new form appeared called knickerbockers, which were adopted for country wear. The legs were cut loose and gathered into a kneeband buckled below the knee. At first they were doubtfully received. 'Met an unconscionable guy in knickerbockers en suite . . . it is wonderful how men do disfigure their appearance nowadays.' (Rev. B. J. Armstrong: *A Norfolk Diary*, 1863). Nevertheless, they grew in popularity and continued into the 20th century.

Of neck-wear, large ties tied in a bow and the shoe-tie 'not half so broad as a watch ribbon' were both worn in the 1850s. Scarf ties filling the front gap and worn with a tie pin were popular. The octagon tie was a favourite from the 1860s on. It was a made-up scarf arranged octagonally, worn with a tie pin and suspended from a neck band fastened behind. Shirt collars varied in shape and height, reaching about three inches in 1899: 'certainly more than the average man can wear with comfort.' (*The Tailor and Cutter*).

As negligée, dressing gowns were worn morning or evening for comfort. The smoking jacket was introduced in the 1850s and the breakfast jacket in the 1870s.

Norfolk jacket, knickerbockers and peaked cap (1905)

Outdoors, overcoats tended to be looser and more comfortable, and a large number of styles was produced, of which the more important were: the top frock, a looser form of the frock-coat; the Chesterfield, also loose and large, sometimes having a fly front closure, and given a ticket pocket, in 1859, placed above the coat pocket on the right side; the Inverness, a large, loose overcoat with a deep arm-length cape; and the Ulster, a belted overcoat with a detachable hood sometimes replaced in the 1870s by a short cape. A ticket pocket was inserted in the left sleeve just above the cuff in 1875. Cloaks were usual for evening dress.

Boots and shoes continued as in the previous chapter, but in the 1870s button boots 'have entirely superseded Wellingtons, and Hessians are now only seen at levées.' (*Fashion Then and Now*, 1878). Spats or short gaiters became fashionable from the 1870s on. For evening dress, patent-leather button boots or pumps were the vogue by the end of the century.

A great variety of hats were worn. The top hat, called the silk hat in the 1890s, was now dress wear. The bowler hat, called in the trade a round-crown hard felt and in America known as the Derby hat, gained in popularity from the 1860s on. Other hats were the Homburg, a stiff felt with dented crown; the wide-awake with low crown and wide brim; and the straw hat, the hat with no class distinction. Peaked caps, deer-stalkers and glengarries were worn in the country.

Women, second half of the 19th century

The 1850s and 1860s
England was now entering on a phase of great prosperity, and 'extravagance in dress is one of the prevailing vices of the day' was a cry constantly heard.

In 1851 the American lady Mrs Bloomer came to England to try to persuade English women to adopt a more rational costume, in the form of loose frilled trousers gathered in at the ankles. These became known as bloomers. The name survived, but the garment did not, being considered immodest and unladylike.

Dresses, in the 1850s, often had two bodices to one skirt, the day bodice usually being in the form of a basqued jacket with wide bell sleeves and engageantes, or sleeves of various shapes closed at the wrist. The evening bodice had a low off-the-shoulders décolletage, sloping to a point in front, with short sleeves. But the dominating feature of this period until the end of the 1860s was the cage crinoline, a hooped petticoat distended by whale-bone, and later watch-spring, hoops. By the middle fifties the crinoline had expanded to such a size that 'a firm in Sheffield has taken an order for 40 tons of rolled steel for crinoline' (*The Times*, July, 1857). 'I only wish you could have seen the dress of Lady Wallace. Last night she absolutely could not sit down in an armchair till she had lifted her hoop over the arm on both sides.' (*The Letter-bag of Lady E. Spencer-Stanhope*, 1856).

From about 1865 the fullness receded towards the back once more,

121

producing what was known once again in 1868 as the Grecian Bend. Evening dresses might have slight trains, but for walking the skirts were ankle-length, and in the 1860s the skirt was often hitched up to display a scarlet petticoat, a fashion very popular with young women.

Skirts hitched up on spreading frame,
Petticoats are bright as flame,
Dainty high-heeled boots proclaim
Fast Young Ladies.

(Popular song, 1860)

Caricature of the size of the crinoline (1858)

LEFT Demure bonnets and flounced skirts; the dress on the right
has a jacket bodice (1850)

During the crinoline period, outdoor garments were of necessity wide.
There were mantles with different names and designs, some with hoods,
such as 'the highland cloak . . . measures 16 yards round the edge and
falls in graceful folds', worn for 'excursions'. Some mantles or cloaks
had loose sleeves. Large shawls were also worn. The paletot, waisted
or tent-like, was an overcoat.

Of head-wear, indoor caps, small and white, were still worn, though
by 1855 they were largely discarded by young women who wore instead
a piece of ribbon or, in the 1860s, a hair net of black or coloured chenille
or silk over the chignon. 'Young married ladies need not wear caps until
they acquire the endearing name of "Mother"' (1857). For evening
wear, flowers, ribbon and ornaments were added.

Out of doors, bonnets tied under the chin, the brim framing the face,
were the most usual. In the 1860s the brim rose above the forehead,
forming what was known as the spoon bonnet. After 1864 the shape
was flattened. An ugly (1848–64) was an extra, flexible brim worn round
the bonnet brim to shade the face from the sun. Hats were becoming

123

Crinoline dress with pagoda sleeves and engageantes;
lace shawl (1861)

<small>LEFT</small> Evening dresses, 1860

more popular, especially with young women, but they were not supposed to be worn on Sundays and were considered improper in church. From 1864 glengarry Scotch caps and pork-pie hats were very popular. During the 1850s and 1860s hat trimming was restrained, consisting of a feather, a few flowers or ribbon. Ribbon streamers hanging down behind were very popular and generally known as 'follow-me-lads'.

Hair styles were fairly plain in the 1850s, the hair being smoothed down from a centre parting to a large bun behind, or sometimes looped round the ears. For evening wear, drooping curls were added. The chignon dominated the 1860s. This was sometimes ready-made and could be fixed on with a comb. The American fashion of leaving the back hair to hang down loose over the shoulders began to be adopted

Outdoor garments, spoon bonnets and pork-pie hats (1861)

by some in 1868, and became popular with young women in the next decade.

Footwear included boots and shoes, but boots were usual for outdoor wear and side-lacing silk boots were worn on dressy occasions. 'As for thin shoes, except for dancing they appear to have vanished from the female toilet' (*Punch*, 1859). Plain white stockings were usual with shoes, coloured ones with boots.

The 1870s to the end of the century
The construction of women's dresses was now so complicated that it baffled description even by contemporary experts and, except for the 'house dress', which consisted of a plain high-necked blouse and skirt, all dresses were overloaded with trimming, most had over-skirts variously draped, and trains were usual even for walking or tennis until 1880. 'I

Short polonaise, bustled behind, producing the 'Grecian bend' (1868)

have lost much faith I once had in the common sense and even in the personal delicacy of the present race of average English women by seeing how they will allow their dresses to sweep the streets.' (John Ruskin, 1876). Overtrimming was put down to the 'facilities afforded by the sewing machine' (the chain stitch being used from 1858, the lock-stitch from 1860, by dressmakers). A mixture of colours and materials in the same dress added to the complexity. 'Neither flowers nor rainbows can shew such colours as are worn now by our fashionable girls.' (*Punch*, 1876).

The Dolly Varden dress of 1871 in the polonaise style, that is with short bunched-up overskirt attached to the bodice, was always made of chintz or cretonne with a bright cotton or silk petticoat (i.e. skirt).

Until *c* 1878 the skirt was expanded behind by means of the crinolette, a form of under-petticoat with hoops at the back only. Then, starting in 1874, skirts became sheath-like to the ground, the front being tied back underneath by pairs of tapes to flatten it. These dresses, known as tie-backs, were so pulled in during the four years 1878–82 that 'a fashionable lady waddling along was barely able to move her feet six inches at a time.'

All through the 1880s drapery continued, but walking-skirts were without trains. The most conspicuous feature of this decade was the large bustle, which finally disappeared in 1889.

The most fashionable outdoor garment through the 1870s and 1880s was the dolman, whose shawl-like sleeves limited the mobility of the arms to such an extent that with one style 'a lady could scarcely blow her nose' (1881). Cloaks and overcoats were also worn.

Indoor caps ceased to be worn by young women, and by 1887 they were also discarded by married women, but they were still occasionally worn by old ladies up to the end of the century.

Out of doors, the social significance of the bonnet was losing its importance, and there were 'American young women who regarded the hat almost symbolic of emancipation' (1880). The bonnet was often only

The Dolly Varden costume (1871)

RIGHT A ball dress in the tie-back style (1879)

FAR RIGHT Trained tie-back walking costumes (1876)

distinguished from the hat by being tied under the chin. In the 1870s hats and bonnets were small, with the exception of a few wide-brimmed hats, such as the Dolly Varden or shepherdess hat, worn perched forward on account of the large chignon then in vogue. The gable bonnet of the 1880s formed a pointed arch over the face, as did the gable toque. The Jubilee year of 1887 saw 'a perfect war between high and flat crowns' for hats, one of the high crowned being called the 'three storeys and a basement' hat. There was a strange fashion during this decade for trimming hats and some evening dresses with dead animals. The following are examples: a whole aviary of birds and nests with eggs, beetles, cockchafers, scorpions, rats, mice, snakes, spiders, flies, cats' heads, caterpillars, 'and even lizards and toads' (1885).

Hair styles in the 1870s became very elaborate. The chignon, coiled, plaited or in roll curls, spread up from the neck to the top of the head, while the front hair was often brushed back over a pad or worn with a low 'frizzed' fringe. Much artificial hair was necessary and made-up toupees called 'frizzettes' were common. In 1870 a single firm was turning out two tons of frizzettes a week. Throughout the 1880s hair

Evening dress with
large bustle (1885)

L et boundless love, for aye serene,
O nce reach the heart, forsakes it no[...]
U nquenched, unutterable, unseen,
I t bides both fair and fickle weather[...]
S o beauty gains a grace from the [...]

Bustled dolman-pelisses
and 'three storeys and a
basement' hats (1886)

was dressed 'very simple and close to the head, shewing all the outlines'
(1880).

By the end of this decade the need for costumes suitable for outdoor
exercise was at last being recognised, and through the 1890s great strides
were made. The increasing popularity of outdoor activities, thanks
especially to the advent of the bicycle, made more practical costumes
inevitable.

With day dresses (except for afternoon and summer dresses), tailor-
mades and their equivalents reigned supreme. Bodices were shaped to
the figure, or a loose blouse might be worn. Sleeves gradually expanded
to a huge leg-of-mutton shape, which vanished abruptly in 1897. Subsequently sleeves were close-fitting, sometimes having a small shoulder
puff.

The new gored skirts of the 1890s were different from any predecessors
in that the goring was carried up to the waist without any gathering.
The excessive drapery of the 1880s was discarded, as was the over-skirt
after 1894.

Evening dresses followed the general pattern of day dresses, but skirts
were generally trained and up to *c* 1897 violent colour contrasts were

Family group
of 1883, showing
older woman
wearing lace cap

popular—yellow being a favourite—and a craze for jet trimmings came in. 'The more jet you introduce on a dinner gown, the more fashionable' (1895).

Out of doors the three-quarter-length overcoat, loose or figure-fitting, was worn throughout this decade, but owing to the size of the gigot sleeves, which often required sleeve-tongs to pull them through coat sleeves, cloaks were equally fashionable. These were waist- or thigh-length and usually made with upstanding collars in the Medici style. The bolero, a very short jacket worn over a blouse, was popular with young women.

Indoor head-wear had vanished except for old ladies, who still sometimes wore small oval lace caps raised in front. Outdoors small bonnets and toques were worn, perched on the top of the head 'as if intended for a big doll'. They were identical in shape, but the bonnet had strings. 'Such a convenient fashion, for they can be adapted to young and old' (1893). A crown in the shape of an hour-glass was very popular.

The Homburg hat was worn throughout, but other hats varied, tending to be rather small with upright trimming arranged in vertical sprays of flowers, ribbons, lace aigrettes, feathers and birds. 'Some twenty to thirty million dead birds are imported into this country annually to supply the demands of murderous millinery' (1895).

Hair was worn with a curly fringe, or brushed back into a 'bun' worn high or at the nape of the neck. The 'door knocker' or 'tea-pot-handle' style, with a projecting loop from a coil high at the back of the head, was very fashionable from 1896.

Shoes, laced in front, and boots, laced or buttoned, had rounded toes until 1898, when the American pointed toes came into fashion for all footwear. Evening slippers had Louis heels. Stockings were black, though in summer white or coloured ones were permissible. Evening stockings were usually of black silk or coloured to match the dress.

The obvious use of rouge or scent was at this time incorrect for the gentlewoman.

Mention must finally be made of the bicycling costume. This was a short coat and skirt with blouse, or waistcoat bodice, and a cap, or small felt or sailor hat. But instead of skirts the more venturesome young women wore knickerbockers, also called rationals. 'Strange doubts possessed him as to the nature of her nether costume . . . the things were . . . yes! . . . rationals!' (H. G. Wells: *The Wheels of Chance*, 1896).

The 'New Woman' in
cycling costume
(1895–1900)

Tailor-made costumes
with gored skirts, and a
golf cape (1894)

The first half of the 20th century

Men

Men's suits remained essentially unchanged until the fateful August, 1914. The morning coat was, however, replacing the frock-coat, which by 1921 was said to be as 'dead as the Dodo'. Coats tended to be somewhat short-waisted, and a white slip within the waistcoat of the frock and morning coat was fashionable. Lounge suits, especially in striped flannel, were, however, becoming the usual day wear. Trousers were narrow, and in 1912 the bottoms of the legs in lounge suits were permanently turned up.

Frock-coat and morning coat, both worn with striped trousers (1913)

133

Plus-fours suit with Fair
Isle pullover (1925)

Smart lounge suit with well-marked
trouser crease and bottoms turned up, worn
with bowler hat and spats (1914)

Out of doors, hats were always worn in town, but the bowler and the
Homburg hat were replacing the silk top hat. The sack overcoat was
preferred to a fitting style.

After the first world war, according to *The Tailor and Cutter*, all that
survived was 'a costume of dull drab monotony and severe cut and
outline that offends the aesthetic faculty and repels and depresses.' But
colour was soon introduced by the Fair Isle pullover, and novelties in
leg-wear were the long full golfer's knickerbockers called plus-fours,
which became popular in 1925.

Spats were still worn with morning coats in town, but after 1918 the

Flared, trained skirt—
visiting costume,
1903

principal change was towards abandoning formality. Hats, gloves and waistcoats were often omitted and formal costume for special occasions was often hired.

Women

Feminine fashions during the Edwardian period emphasised curves, with tight waists and flared bell-shaped skirts sweeping the ground and often trained, even for walking dresses. The adoption of the straight-fronted corset, thought to be less injurious to health than the tight-waisted ones of the 1880s and 1890s, gave the figure a forward tilt so that the lady assumed a 'swan-like' posture. Colours were soft, materials delicate, and fragile trimmings were very popular. From 1909 the close-fitting tubular dress with long hobble skirt appeared, and hats became enormous. 'The Parisian elegante has adapted her walk to a waddle, and presents the strangest spectacle, crowned by a hat of mammoth dimen-

135

LEFT 'Simple toilette for spring wear': dress with underbodice and hobble skirt (1911)

CENTRE Informal two-piece costume and cloche hat (1926)

RIGHT Victor Stiebel suits for country wear (1936)

sions and gradually dwindling off at her feet. Her similitude to a peg top is unmistakable.' This was a contemporary comment. Variations of this line were worn until even after the beginning of the first world war, though slit skirts replaced the tight 'hobble' and hats grew smaller.

The first world war necessitated more practical garments with fuller and shorter skirts. There was tremendous contrast between the sensible, almost drab tailor-made clothes worn for the working day and the gaily coloured low-cut evening dresses. Materials, corsets and fastenings were in short supply and a looser, straighter and more simple line prevailed. Dress hems descended again to the ankle just after the war, but after almost annual fluctuations in length they were shortened to the knee in 1925–26. It was fashionable to look young, slim and boyish, and post-war fashions culminated in the juvenile style described as 'such enchanting, sexless, bosomless, hipless, thighless creatures', with short hair and

Evening dresses, 1935

low waistlines. Cloche hats, pulled down almost to the eyebrows, were the rage.

By 1929 there was a return to femininity with 'fashion's new discovery that the feminine form is lovely', and the less boyish, more curvacious figure was emphasised by dresses which were longer, cut on the cross, and with an emphasis at the natural waist. Trim tailored clothes were popular for day with hem lines fluctuating between calf and knee length and at their shortest just before the second world war. Sleeves were an important fashion feature, becoming full at the upper arm in 1934–7, and by the eve of war in 1938–9 shoulders had become very broad and square cut. Hats, handbags and stockings, now usually beige and not matching the dress as in the 1920s, were significant accessories. Evening dresses were long and often low-backed, and in 1938 women were told 'you can be unbelievably alluring in the sheathlike evening frock.'

Then, with the second world war, shortages of materials and government controls on quality and price made 'utility' both the law and the fashion, and economy rather than ostentation the ideal. Trousers were extensively worn, thus fulfilling a remarkable prophecy made by a magazine in 1892 that 'in fifty years, women will be wearing trousers.'

Not until 1949 did all garments become coupon-free again. But 1947 heralded a sterling and welcome revival: once more feminity returned, with the New Look, introduced from Paris and distinguished by more gently curving shoulders, a tighter waist and a longer skirt. Subsequent cycles are beyond the scope of this book.

Having traced the changing fashions through many centuries, I will end by quoting Beaumont and Fletcher, who in the Prologue to *The Noble Gentleman* (1647) wrote:

> Nothing is thought rare
> Which is not new, and follow'd;
>   yet we know
> That what was worn some twenty
>   years ago
> Comes into grace again.

Select Bibliography

ARNOLD, J. and ANTHONY, P. *Costume, a general bibliography*; Costume Society, Bury, Lancs. 1977

ARNOLD, J. *A Handbook of Costume*; Methuen, London, 1978 and S. G. Phillips, New York, 1974

BLUM, S. (ed.) *Ackermann's Costume Plates: Women's Fashions in England 1818–28*; Dover, London and New York, 1979

BUCK, A. *Dress in the Eighteenth Century*; Batsford, London and Holmes & Meier, New York, 1979

BYRDE, P. *The Male Image*; Batsford, London, 1977

CARTER, E. *The Changing World of Fashion, 1900 to the Present*; Weidenfeld, London and Putnam, New York, 1977

CUNNINGTON, C. W. & P. *A Handbook of English Costume in the Sixteenth Century*; Faber, London and Plays Inc., Boston, 1970
– *A Handbook of English Costume in the Seventeenth Century*; as above, 1973
– *A Handbook of English Costume in the Eighteenth Century*; as above, 1972
– *A Handbook of English Costume in the Nineteenth Century*; as above, 1970
– *A Handbook of English Mediaeval Costume*; Faber, London, 1952

CUNNINGTON, P. and LUCAS, C. *Occupational Costume in England from the Eleventh Century to 1914*; A. & C. Black, London, 1967 and Humanities Press, Atlantic Highlands, N.J., 1976

CUNNINGTON, P. and MANSFIELD, A. *English Costume for Sports and Outdoor Recreations*, 16th–19th Century; A. & C. Black, London and Humanities Press, Atlantic Highlands, N.J., 1969
– *A Handbook of English Costume in the Twentieth Century*; Faber, London and Plays, Inc., Boston, 1973

DAVENPORT, M. *The Story of Costume*; Crown, New York, 1968

EWING, E. *Dress and Undress: A History of Women's Underwear*; Batsford, London 1977 and Drama Book Specialists, New York, 1978
– *A History of Children's Costume*; Batsford, London, 1977 and Scribners, New York, 1978
– *A History of Twentieth Century Fashion*; Batsford, London, 1978 and Scribners, New York, 1975

GINSBURG, M. *The Art of Fashion 1600–1939*; HMSO, London
– *An Introduction to Fashion Illustration*; Victoria and Albert Museum/Pitman, London 1980

GLYNN, P. with GINSBURG, M. *In Fashion: Dress in the Twentieth Century*; Allen & Unwin, London and Oxford University Press, New York, 1978

LAVER, J. *A Concise History of Costume*; Thames & Hudson, London, 1969 and Scribners, New York, 1974

WAUGH, N. *The Cut of Men's Clothes, 1600–1914*; Faber, London and Theatre Arts, New York, 1977

YARWOOD, D. *Encyclopedia of World Costume*; Batsford, London and Scribners, New York, 1978

Acknowledgements

First edition: the author wishes to express her thanks to those people who so kindly helped in the selecting and checking of illustrations; in particular to her daughter, Mrs Luckham, to Major Mansfield and, above all, to Miss Catherine Lucas who gave up so much of her time to this work.

Second edition (revised with the assistance of Madeleine Grinsburg): the author and publishers gratefully acknowledge the following sources from which reproductions have been taken:

The portraits of Henry VIII and his Family, artist unknown, (detail) on page 30 and 'Young Man in Red', German School, on page 32 are reproduced by gracious permission of Her Majesty the Queen.

PAGE

frontispiece: 'Ready for the party' by James Hayllar, 1861; by courtesy of Christie's

8, 9 From Strutt's *A Complete View of the Dress*

Index